TH
OF

Raymond Edwards
and
Mgr John Armitage

*All booklets are published
thanks to the generosity of the supporters
of the Catholic Truth Society*

Contents

PART I

England as Mary's Dowry: its Meaning and History
by Raymond Edwards

PART II

Devotion to Our Lady in England
by Mgr John Armitage

Image page 26: Dowry Painting of Our Lady of Walsingham *by Amanda de Pulford.*

All rights reserved. First published 2020 by The Incorporated Catholic Truth Society, 40-46 Harleyford Road, London SE11 5AY. Tel: 020 7640 0042 Fax: 020 7640 0046. © 2020 The Incorporated Catholic Truth Society. www.ctsbooks.org

ISBN 978 1 78469 632 0

On 29th March 2020, the Bishops of England will formally rededicate our country as the Dowry of Mary. This will take place in cathedrals, parishes, schools and religious houses; where people are not able to attend a public dedication, they may make their own commemoration at home or wherever they may be.

To many Catholics, and probably to most non-Catholics, this may seem a curious thing for our bishops to do, and to invite us to take part in. But it is worth taking a moment to understand the history and theology of this event before passing it over with only a raised eyebrow. This pamphlet tries to answer some obvious and reasonable questions we may have about the Dowry of Mary. It also says something about its place in English history, and in the devotional life of the people of England for centuries.

PART I

ENGLAND AS MARY'S DOWRY: ITS MEANING AND HISTORY

In common usage, insofar as it is a word in common usage these days, a **dowry** (a word that stems from the same root that gives us the word **endowment**) is normally thought of as a gift (perhaps of property, but more usually money) that accompanies a woman on her marriage: it is a transfer of wealth from the wife's family to her and her husband on their marriage. Nineteenth century novels are full of the complex, difficult or competitive circumstances that might arise from a young woman's possession of, or need for, a handsome dowry.

This is not the sense of the word we are dealing with here.

Under English common law, and some other legal systems, a dowry might be something else altogether: not a gift from the wife's family to the married couple to accompany wife-to-be, but instead a gift from the husband to his wife on the occasion of their marriage. It would normally be a substantial property settled on her and under her sole legal control; its primary purpose was to allow her financial independence in the event she should become a widow, rather than having to rely on the good will of her deceased husband's family.

Historically, the terms **dower** and **dowry** are variants of the same word, and are used indifferently in both these senses.[1] Contemporary usage however tends to distinguish **dowry** "property brought by the bride to her husband on marriage" (so, a transfer of property from the wife's parents to the new household), from **dower**, "property assigned by a husband to his wife, usually on their wedding day, for her maintenance in widowhood". This second sense is particularly important under English law, where women (unlike those living under most continental legal systems) could own property in their own right, independent of their husbands. English law was careful to define and protect the rights of property held as dower, which a husband was unable to touch nor was it liable for any debts to be discharged at his death. Various different types of dower were recognised by law; almost all of them were abolished by Act of Parliament in the nineteenth century.

However, this usage survives in the word **dowager**, "woman whose husband is dead and enjoys a title or property derived from him": as, for instance, the Dowager Duchess of Loamshire. Habitual visitors to historic

---

[1] AN *dowarie*, OF *douaire*, MedL *dotarium* cl Lat *dos, dot-* "dowry" from *dotare*, "endow". C.T. Onions (*Oxford Dictionary of English Etymology*) has **dowry** s.xiv (R. Mannyng) "money that a wife brings her husband"; and **dower** also s.xiv, "dowry" in same sense (Chaucer, Clerk's Tale IV.807, "'and thilke dowere that ye broghten me / Taak it agayn; I graunte it of my grace. / Retourneth to youre fadres hous,' quod he.", and 30 lines later (IV.848) **dowaire** in the same sense). Onions also gives an obsolete sense of **dower** (s.xiv), "portion of a deceased husband's estate allowed to a widow".

properties will have come across the occasional **Dower House**, which is normally a smaller house within the estate of a larger one where such a widow might live.

If we say that England is Mary's Dowry, then, we are saying that our country is (in some sense) in a particular way dedicated to the Virgin Mary, and is her own and inalienable possession, given over to her for her exclusive use.

Where does it come from?

Whilst there is some evidence for it in medieval times, the modern use of the title Dowry of Mary for England dates from 1893.

In May 1893, the Bishops of England, led by the then Archbishop of Westminster, Herbert Cardinal Vaughan, issued a pastoral letter announcing that, at the suggestion of the Pope, Leo XIII, they proposed to renew the ancient dedication of England to two of its sometime primary patrons, the Virgin Mary and St Peter.

The Pope had suggested this in February that year, in his response to an address presented to him by a group of English pilgrims who had come to Rome to congratulate Leo on the fiftieth anniversary of his being made a bishop. The group was led by the Duke of Norfolk, then as now England's premier Catholic layman, but was presented to Leo by Cardinal Vaughan, who had arrived in Rome the previous month to be made Cardinal at the consistory.

Vaughan had been made Archbishop of Westminster on 29th March 1892; part of that entailed receiving a pallium from the Pope. Vaughan might have travelled to Rome and received it in person; instead, eager to celebrate his enthronement in an English setting, he was enthroned on 8th May 1892, at the then pro-cathedral of Our Lady of Victories in Kensington. But when made Cardinal, he was happy to travel to Rome to be invested, and to prolong his stay to take in the Pope's anniversary celebrations.

This accounts for the presence of Cardinal Vaughan, the Duke of Norfolk and miscellaneous English pilgrims in Rome that February. But it does not explain why the Pope made this suggestion. It seems unlikely that Leo XIII should have come up with the notion of the renewal of England's ancient dedication to the Virgin Mary wholly unprompted. The simplest explanation would be to suppose that Vaughan had introduced the idea at some point in the previous month, and that Leo was happy to make the suggestion his own.

Supposing this to be true, we then need to ask where Vaughan might have come across the idea. Herbert Vaughan was of course eldest son of an old recusant family, the Vaughans of Courtfield, and if there was any context where memory of this old title might have lingered, it might have been amongst such people. But he need not have looked back so far. A book had appeared only seventeen years previously that, had he noticed it, would have brought it firmly to his attention. We do not know for sure that Vaughan read it, but it was several times reprinted; a revised edition had appeared as recently as 1890.

In 1875, then, an English Redemptorist, Fr Thomas Bridgett, published a book titled *Our Lady's Dowry: How England Gained and Lost that Title*.[2] It is a historical study of Marian devotion in England, with particular focus on the title The Dowry of Mary (Dos Mariae, Our Lady's Dowry, Mary's Dowry, The Dower of Mary and similar variants). Bridgett cites various seventeenth century writers who mention it as "a former title of England"; at least two of the English seminaries in Spain had paintings, presumably of sixteenth century or later date, showing the Virgin Mary extending her protection to England, or to English seminarians, and one of them explicitly stated *Anglia dos Mariae*, "England is Mary's dowry".[3] The title is certainly used in the fifteenth century. The English army before Agincourt, according to the contemporary source Thomas Elmham, asked the intercession of Mary, protectress of her

---

[2] The 1875 text I have seen describes itself as the second edition, but I have seen no earlier date for this text.

[3] St Gregory's Seminary in Seville had a painting of Our Lady with arms outstretched over the heads of English seminarians with the inscription, *Anglia Dos Mariae*, "England is the Dowry of Mary". At the base of the picture there is a further Latin inscription that reads, in translation: *Britain, once converted, was the first one to give the sceptre to Our Lady's Son, and from then on England has been known as the Dowry of Mary. Thus, we give back the gift, Holy Mother, and pray you to defend, mercifully and with justice all those who are trying to recover it.*

dower. His verse account of Henry V's life has the English army at Agincourt's battle-cry

Virgo Maria fave, propria pro dote; Georgi
Miles, et Edwarde, rex pie, confer opem.

Literally, this is "O Virgin Mary, support your own dowry; George the knight, and Edward, holy king, grant your help." Fr Thomas Bridgett rendered it "Our Lady for her Dowry; St George and St Edward to our aid!" which seems a fair guess at how it might have run in English.[4]

Earlier still, in 1399 (or more probably 1400), the Archbishop of Canterbury, Thomas Arundel, had in a letter to his fellow bishops named England as Mary's Dowry. We will come back to Arundel later.

So much for some attestations.
But where did it originate?

The idea of a dowry or dower, as we have seen, implies a gift; and, in this case, the gift of an entire country. The only authority able to make the gift of a country is, in pre-modern terms, the monarch; so we are looking, in all likelihood, for something done, and probably done formally, by a king of England.

Some writers have suggested that the title is ultimately of Anglo-Saxon date, perhaps eleventh century, and instituted by Edward the Confessor. There is exactly no evidence

---

[4] See Bridgett in *Historical Papers* (London, Catholic Truth Society, 1894), pp.166-167.

for this statement. Certainly, Anglo-Saxon England had a strong and developed theology and practice of Marian devotion – the feast of the (immaculate) conception of the Virgin Mary was celebrated in England, uniquely in Western Europe, by the early eleventh century, and survived the deliberate efforts of the Normans to suppress it. Celebration of this feast spread from England to the rest of Western Christendom.[5] But the projection into a pre-Conquest past of the title Dowry of Mary seems wholly fanciful, another instance of the Anglo-Saxon origin myths beloved of English antiquarians (who have confected similar imaginary pedigrees for the process of trial by jury, and indeed parliamentary procedure as a whole).

The earliest identified use of this title seems to be in about 1350 by John Lathbury, a Franciscan theologian, in his well-known commentary on Lamentations:[6] "it is commonly said that the land of England is Mary's dowry".[7] One historian suggests this may be seen in the context of an effort made by the king, Edward III, in the 1350s to extend the range of England's patron saints. As well as a

---

[5] See the essay by Edmund Bishop, reprinted in his *Liturgica Historica* (Oxford, Clarendon Press, 1918), pp.238-259, and the summary of Bishop's work in Nigel Abercrombie, *The Life and Work of Edmund Bishop* (London, Longmans, 1959), p.108.

[6] See Nigel Saul, *For Honour and Fame: Chivalry in England 1066-1500* (London, Random House, 2011), p.208. For Lathbury, see Beryl Smalley, *English Friars and Antiquity* (Oxford, Blackwell, 1960) pp.221-239, and A.G. Little, *The Greyfriars in Oxford* (Oxford, Oxford Historical S,ociety, 1892), pp.235-236.

[7] *Dicitur enim vulgariter quod terra Anglie est dos Marie.* (Smalley, op. cit. p.223)

renewed emphasis on St George (previously claimed as patron by, amongst others, the French kings), royal art of these middle decades of the century (the wall paintings in St Stephen's chapel in Westminster, for example, and the Great Seal made around 1360) portray the Virgin Mary as protectress of the realm, alongside St George.[8]

The wall paintings in St Stephen's chapel are worth noting. We now think of the Palace of Westminster as a synonym for Parliament, but it was for centuries primarily a royal palace; Parliament, when it was summoned, would meet in one of its chambers, or nearby in the Abbey. The main chapel of the Palace of Westminster was dedicated to St Stephen; there was a smaller lady chapel annexed to it.

In the immediate aftermath of the English Reformation, Edward VI (Henry VIII's strongly Protestant son) had these chapels converted to chambers where Parliament might meet. The existing walls, which were painted, were covered with oak panelling. This panelling remained in place until 1800. In that year, after the Act of Union joined the English and Irish Parliaments together, the Parliament chamber needed to be enlarged. In the course of this, the sixteenth century oak panelling was taken down, and the medieval wall paintings were discovered, and observed

---

[8] See Nigel Saul, op. cit., pp.206-212. Edward III made St George patron of the Order of the Garter in the 1340s, and founded a priestly college at Windsor to make intercession to St George. It is at this time that he begins to be portrayed alongside England's long-standing patrons St Edward the Confessor and St Edmund, King and Martyr.

to be in excellent condition. Contemporary reports state that, behind the Speaker's chair, there was a painting of the Virgin and Child, with St Joseph; King Edward III, his queen, and their children were also shown, making an offering to Our Lady.

Fr Bridgett speculated that

> It may either have commemorated an historical event, or its execution may be considered an historical event in itself. It is not, nor does it record an act of private devotion... Acolytes were holding lighted tapers and two angels were represented as taking part in a solemnity. It is the consecration of England, through its Sovereign to the Blessed Virgin. It was before the eyes of every King and noble until hidden by Edward VI.

This is certainly possible, but cannot be asserted as fact without further evidence. Unfortunately, these wall paintings were destroyed, along with the great majority of the medieval fabric of the palace, in the great fire of 1834.

In any event, it was clearly likely that particular marks and titles of Marian devotion were receiving royal encouragement. However, there is no particular event that has yet been identified as the occasion of a formal dedication.

This official encouragement of Marian devotion reached a further level in the following reign.

Richard II

Most writers examining the question of England as Our Lady's Dowry have focussed on the reign of Richard II, and his apparent devotion to the Virgin under her title of Our Lady of Pew. The Lady Chapel in the Palace of Westminster (the main royal residence, just up river from the City of London) was dedicated to her under this title.

The monks of Westminster had for some time asserted a claim to jurisdiction over the royal chapels in the Palace of Westminster, which included the chapel of Our Lady of Pew. In the early 1370s, however, this claim was finally rejected; the monks no longer had access to the royal chapels, which were now reserved for the canons of the Chapel of St Stephen and the other chapels within the palace.

In 1377, the countess of Pembroke endowed a chantry chapel in Westminster Abbey to have Masses sung for her dead husband. This "chapel" was little more than a niche, but it was immediately next to the Abbey's chapel of St John the Baptist (who was one of the king's patron saints). The countess donated an alabaster statue of the Virgin Mary to stand in her chantry; the then Abbot of Westminster, a larger-than-life figure named Nicholas Litlington, named the statue, and thus the nascent Lady Chapel, Our Lady of Pew, after the shrine in the palace.[9] This was both a means of allowing a particular devotion to continue for the monastic community, and (perhaps) a barbed response to the officious clergy of the palace.

The title "Our Lady of Pew" is a curious one. No wholly satisfactory etymology for the name exists; perhaps the most plausible derives it from Notre Dame Puissant, anglicised as Pewssant, meaning Virgo Potens, Our Lady of Power. Others have suggested Notre Dame de Puits, although without explaining what particular wells are alluded to, or why; or perhaps from the French shrine of Our Lady of Puy.[10]

Whatever the origin of this title, clearly her cult was a popular one, enough to warrant establishing a dedicated chapel when the original became inaccessible. One of

---

[9] The statue disappeared, probably at the time of the Reformation; it was replaced in 1971 by a copy of the medieval alabaster statue of the Virgin now in Westminster Cathedral, where it is called Our Lady of Westminster: that statue was enthroned in the cathedral in 1955, after it was bought from a French dealer. It is English alabaster work, but a good deal of that was made for the export market. The copy now in Westminster Abbey was made by a Catholic nun of Minster Abbey; on the back of the statue she inscribed *Ut unum sint*: "that they may be one".

[10] Le Puy-en-Velay, in the Haute-Loire department in Auvergne, is an ancient centre of Marian pilgrimage (Charlemagne was an early pilgrim). The town is now perhaps best known for its eponymous lentil. Like much else, Puy's Marian shrine was destroyed in the French Revolution. It contained an ebony statue of the Virgin given by St Louis, king of France. This suggests that the usual image of Notre Dame de Puy might have been a black-skinned Madonna, common in many parts especially of southern France. The white-skinned Virgin of the Wilton Diptych, if she is indeed Our Lady of Pew, would thus tend to argue against any such close connexion between Our Lady of the Pew and Notre Dame de Puy, but it is possible that the title was borrowed without the appearance.

those who had a strong devotion to Our Lady of Pew was the new king, Richard II.

Richard II has a mixed press. On the one hand, his reign was culturally rich beyond the norm of medieval English kingship: Chaucer, Gower, and the Gawain poet all write in his reign, at least two of them within his court circle. Westminster Hall was rebuilt by him (supervised in part by Chaucer, in fact); the one unchallenged masterpiece of late medieval English painting, the Wilton Diptych, was made for the king, and indeed portrays him. We shall return to this picture later.

On the other hand, his reign was politically chaotic, and ended in him being deposed by his cousin, Henry of Bolingbroke, who assumed the throne in 1399 as Henry IV. Richard died soon thereafter, almost certainly murdered.

Richard succeeded his grandfather, Edward III, in 1377. aged ten; his father, Edward of Woodstock (known to later ages, though not his contemporaries, as the Black Prince) had died the year before, after a protracted illness. Richard was supported, and it may be mostly controlled, by a group of noble advisers. England was still suffering from the social and economic effects of the Black Death a generation before, and the continuing war with France. Taxation was heavy, and fell disproportionately on the poor; particularly resented were a series of "poll taxes", levied on all men without distinction. Much of the money was spent on unsuccessful military expeditions in France; there had not been a major victory of English arms since Najera in 1367, and Poitiers a decade before that.

The Peasants' Revolt

Four years into his reign, Richard was faced with a crisis of monarchy. The proposed poll tax of 1381 led to a popular uprising, known to history as the Peasants' Revolt. A mob from Kent and Essex, including numerous ex-soldiers, gathered at Blackheath, and then invaded London. They sacked and destroyed the Savoy Palace, the greatest nobleman's house in England, which belonged to the king's uncle John of Gaunt (who was blamed for the poll tax). Royal officials were hunted out and lynched. They killed both the Archbishop of Canterbury (who was also Lord Chancellor) and the Lord High Treasurer.

The king resolved to confront the mob in person and, on Saturday 15th June 1381, he rode out with some of his lords from the Tower, where he had taken refuge. They stopped, first, at Westminster Abbey, where the king prayed at the shrine of Our Lady of Pew. Earlier that day, the mob had invaded the Abbey, and dragged from it the keeper of the Marshalsea Prison, who had sought sanctuary there; he was taken to Cheapside, and executed.

The king and his lords went from the Abbey to Smithfield, where the young king confronted the mob. Their leader,

Wat Tyler, became insolent, and was promptly stabbed by the Lord Mayor, William Walworth, who was with the king; the mob was enraged, and prepared to attack them. Then the king rode forward, alone, and confronted them, saying, "Sirs, will you shoot your king? I am your captain, follow me." He then rode off slowly northward, and they followed him. Soon the Lord Mayor arrived with a force of soldiers, and the mob was dispersed. The king refused to allow any violence to be done to them; at Clerkenwell Fields, he stopped and knighted Walworth on the spot. The first great crisis of his reign was over.

There is evidence that the Abbey shrine of Our Lady of Pew was refurbished and embellished at this time, and by the king (since his badge, the white hart, was found amongst the surviving decorations). We may suppose that he did this in thanksgiving for his triumph over the rebels; the chronicler Froissart has him visiting his mother immediately after the events at Smithfield and declaring "now rejoice yourself and thank God, for now it is time. I have this day recovered mine heritage and the realm of England, which I had near lost."[11]

The Dowry in Art

The late Fr Mark Elvins argued that Richard presented his kingdom to the Virgin (under the title Our Lady of Pew,

---

[11] Froissart, *Chroniques* X.124, tr. Lord Berners; quoted in *The Peasants' Revolt of 1381*, sel. & ed. R.B. Dobson (London, Macmillan, 1970), p.198.

hence the refurbished shrine in the Abbey) in thanksgiving for regaining it in 1381, and the title Dos Mariae stems from that. To establish the plausibility of this claim, we need to look at some pictures.

The most famous icon of the Marian piety of Richard II's reign is the Wilton Diptych, an altarpiece now in the National Gallery. Richard II is here one of three kings of England (the others being the two saints Edmund the Martyr, and Edward the Confessor) doing homage to the Virgin and Child. Richard had in fact been born on the feast of the Epiphany in 1367 (and, according to a contemporary chronicler, three kings – of Castile, Navarre, and Portugal – had been present at his birth) which may be reflected here, although John the Baptist is also shown, which spoils the exact echo. The painting is thematically rich, and can probably not be fully explained by a political reading; but it indisputably shows Richard II being presented to the Virgin by his three patrons; she is surrounded by angels, each of whom wears Richard's badge of the white hart (which the king is also wearing), and one of whom carries a banner of St George. This picture could certainly be interpreted as marking the formal donation of the realm of England to the Virgin; but an explicit and unambiguous link is lacking.

There is however evidence of at least one other painting with a comparable theme, but more explicitly linked to the title. There was formerly a painting in the English Hospice of St Thomas in Rome (now the Venerable English College) of a king and queen (very probably Richard II and Anne of Bohemia) presenting England (depicted on a globe or map) to the Virgin, with the inscription *Dos tua, Virgo pia / Haec est; quare rege, Maria*: "Holy Virgin, this is your dowry; and so, Mary, govern it". There are conflicting descriptions of the picture, but it seems to have shown also several saints, including St George and St John (perhaps the Baptist) supporting the king. The painting disappeared in or after 1798, during the French occupation of Rome during their Revolutionary Wars.

The collective evidence of this vanished picture, then, and the extant Wilton Diptych, plus the refurbishment of the shrine of Our Lady of Pew, should be enough to establish Richard's vigorous Marian piety, and the strong likelihood that he made a formal dedication of his realm to the Virgin Mary, most probably in thanksgiving after the events of 1381. From that moment, then, England might be called Our Lady's Dowry as a legal fact, not merely as a pious expression of uncertain origin.

It's now worth mentioning the explicit use of the title Dowry of Mary in the letter written to his fellow bishops by Thomas Arundel, Archbishop of Canterbury. This is usually dated 10th February 1399, but under our current dating it would be 10th February 1400, since the medieval year generally ran from 25th March (the Annunciation) not 1st January. For most of 1399, Thomas Arundel was not Archbishop of Canterbury, but, nominally at least, bishop of the Scottish see of St Andrews. He was a strong opponent of Richard II, and had been Archbishop of Canterbury from 1395-1397, when he was deprived of his see by the king and went into exile; the king arranged for him to be given St Andrews as a consolation, but he clearly reckoned himself wronged.

When Henry Bolingbroke, who was to depose Richard and usurp the throne under the title Henry IV, landed in England with his troops in early 1399 with the aim of seizing the crown, Thomas Arundel was one of the earliest magnates to join him. He was instrumental in persuading Richard to leave his stronghold in Conwy Castle, surrender to Henry's army (under a solemn promise of safe-conduct, which was at once broken), and agree to abdicate. One of the earliest acts of the new king, in return, was to restore Arundel to Canterbury.

It is in this context that we should read the formal letter (or mandate) sent by Arundel to the bishops of his province. He states he is writing at the express request of the king, who is not named; but it can only be Henry, since Arundel was not Archbishop until Richard had been deposed.[12] The text runs, in part,

---

[12] Presumably the mandate was issued as part of the proceedings of the great council summoned by Henry that met on 9th February 1400. Its main purpose was to allow the magnates of the realm, lay and clerical both, to vote money for the king's expenses without the bother and trouble of summoning a Parliament to agree taxation of the commons.

The contemplation of the great mystery of the Incarnation has brought all Christian nations to venerate her from whom came the beginnings of redemption. But we as humble servants of her inheritance, and liegemen of her especial dower, as we are approved by common parlance, ought to excel all others on the favour of our praises and devotions to her.[13]

We have argued above that the title Dowry of Mary is very probably something closely connected with the personal piety of Richard II and his court, and represented his thanksgiving for the restoration of his authority after the perilous events of the Peasants' Revolt. For the new usurping king's leading ecclesiastical ally to use this title in a formal address to the bishops, at the king's explicit request, was (surely) a deliberate and conscious attempt to claim not just the moral and legal legitimacy that had previously belonged to Richard II, but also the panoply of heavenly patronage he had appealed to.

Continued Use of the Title

The Dowry of Mary may have begun as a consciously Ricardian title, but the new regime wished to make it its own. Richard had a high notion of the religious role of a

---

[13] Quoted in Mark Elvins, *Old Catholic England* (London, Catholic Truth Society, 1978), p.3; cf. D. Gordon, "A New Discovery in the Wilton Diptych" in *Burlington Magazine* cxxxiv (1992), p.667 n.22.

king, and of the sacred nature of his office and its anointing. For any usurper to be seen as legitimate, he must arrogate to himself not just the material supports of the office, but also its spiritual buttressing; and this meant not just the goodwill and support of bishops, abbots and so on, but also that of the realm's patron saints, at whose head Richard II had set the Virgin Mary. Much as Edward III had claimed St George and the Virgin Mary's patronage from the kings of France, so now Henry Bolingbroke's regime asserted its claim to the Richard's particular patron of the realm.

Collectively, then, the evidence of pictures together with the fragmentary historical record suggests that insofar as the title Dowry of Mary had official and public status, this stems from a formal act of dedication made by King Richard II, probably at the shrine of Our Lady of Pew in Westminster, and very likely in the immediate aftermath of, or at least as a thanksgiving for, the suppression of the Peasants' Revolt in 1381; and that its continuance was a deliberate act by Richard's successors, the usurper Bolingbroke (Henry IV) and his warrior son, Henry V, to reinforce their claim to legitimacy.

Modern Use by the Popes

Whatever the truth of all this, it remains the case that the title and dedication was formally made by the bishops of the Province of Westminster in 1893, at the suggestion of Pope Leo XIII. This act of itself establishes the title in current Catholic usage, though it has no standing in English law.

Pope Francis, incidentally, is well aware of England's history of Marian devotion. In his message to the Eucharistic Congress in Liverpool in 2018 (Adoremus), he wrote:

> The history of the Church in your lands is marked in no small part by the central place that countless saints have given to the Sacrifice of the Mass. These holy men and women, sometimes even to the point of shedding their blood, have given eloquent and steadfast witness to Christ in devotion to the Blessed Eucharist.
>
> Your martyr forebears in particular, whose sufferings speak not so much of human cruelty as of the serenity and strength given by God's grace in the face of trials, are rightly to be venerated, and the Church in England and Wales must never lose sight of their precious memory.
>
> Remaining faithful to that spiritual legacy requires more than an act of remembrance. You must continue to bear witness to the same Lord and same precious gift of the Eucharist today. For past glories are always a beginning, not an end.
>
> The Lord is calling you still, to go out and bear witness…
>
> I pray that the bishops, clergy, religious and lay faithful, as they come to adore the Lord who is the

Bread of Life, will be inspired to enter more deeply into the mystery of Christ's saving death and resurrection made manifest in the Eucharist, and become ever more aware of God's love proclaimed in the celebration of Holy Mass.

On this special occasion, I entrust all taking part in the Congress, and their families, to the maternal intercession of Our Lady of Walsingham, and I cordially impart my Apostolic Blessing as a pledge of peace and joy in Christ the Lord.

PART II

DEVOTION TO OUR LADY IN ENGLAND

1. Mary's Yes at the Annunciation – Our Response

The Annunciation: Mary's Yes to God

...behold the handmaid of the Lord. Let it be done to me according to your Word.

At the Annunciation, Mary said *yes* to the message of the Angel Gabriel, freely accepting God's will in her life that she would give birth to God's son. Like Mary, we are invited to embrace God's will in our lives.

Mary's *yes* changed the world. *Answer with a word, receive the Word of God. Speak your own word, conceive the divine Word. Breathe a passing word, embrace the eternal Word.* (St Bernard of Clairvaux)

The story of the Annunciation (*Lk* 1:26-38) perfectly describes the route of our spiritual journey: before ever we seek God, he is seeking us and initiates the conversation; but we are hesitant and fearful, as we seek to understand God's will in our life. God reminds us of our experience of his love for us, that *nothing is impossible for God*. If we, like Mary, say yes to God, we will conceive the Word in our heart, and bring Christ's love into our families, communities, and our world, for we shall share her joy that *My soul glorifies the Lord and my spirit rejoices in God my saviour, for the Almighty has done great things for me*.

The Tradition of the Dowry: The Yes of a People

The contemplation of the great mystery of the Incarnation has drawn all Christian nations to venerate her from whom came the first beginnings of our redemption. But we English, being the servants of her special inheritance and her own dowry, as we are commonly called, ought to surpass others in the fervour of our praises and devotions.

Thomas Arundel, Archbishop of Canterbury 1399/1400

Unique among all the nations, the Catholics of England have believed for centuries that their nation is the Dowry of Mary, that England belonged in some special way to Mary, who was seen as the country's protectress and who through her powers of intercession acted as the country's defender and guardian.

In medieval English law, a dowry is something that is set aside for the maintenance of a widow. The historical understanding of England as Mary's Dowry is understood in this sense – that, England has been "set apart" for Mary.

It is a title of England, established by an act of the king, and proclaimed by the Archbishop of Canterbury, which has never been rescinded by monarch or Parliament. Our bishops over the years have consecrated our country to the Mother of God for her prayers and protection, and in reparation for the sins of the past. Pope Leo XIII in 1893 reflected that

> The wonderful love which burnt within the heart of your forefathers and mothers towards the great Mother of God... to whose service they consecrated themselves with such abundant proofs of devotion, that the kingdom itself acquired the singular and highly honourable title of 'Mary's Dowry'.

In 1893, the bishops, at the invitation of Pope Leo XIII, rededicated England and Wales to Our Lady and St Peter at a ceremony in the London Oratory. They requested every Catholic church mark this rededication of England using Acts of Consecration, modelled on the solemn Acts done by the assembled hierarchy at the Oratory, on the Sunday following, which was the feast of the Visitation. These twin consecrations were to be repeated each year: that to the Virgin Mary on Rosary Sunday (the first Sunday in October) and to St Peter on the Sunday that fell within the octave of his feast.

The following prayer was to be used; its conclusion was based on a ninth century Anglo-Saxon prayer to Our Lady from the Book of Cerne.

1893 Prayer of Dedication

O Immaculate Virgin, mother of Our Lord Jesus Christ, mother of grace, and queen of the kingdom of thy Son. Humbly kneeling before thee, we offer thee this country in which we live. It once was thine, before it was robbed of the holy faith; all its children were thy children, and thou wert honoured throughout its length and breadth as its Protectress and its Queen. Again do we consecrate it to thee; again do we dedicate it as thy own Dowry. We offer our own hearts, that their love and service may ever grow and increase.

We offer all our brethren, those multitudes who know thee so little, or know thee not at all. May thy prayer bring back the country's ancient faith. May thy intercession lead us to a closer union with thy divine Son. We consecrate ourselves to him through thee. Obtain for us, and for England thy Dowry, every grace and blessing, O clement, O loving, O sweet Virgin Mary.

V. Pray for us, O holy Mother of God.

R. That we may be made worthy of the promises of Christ.

Let us pray:

Holy Mother of God, Virgin ever blest, O Mary Immaculate, pray for us, intercede for us, disdain not to help us. For we are confident and know for certain that you canst obtain all thou willest from thy Son, Our Lord Jesus Christ, God Almighty, the King of Ages, who liveth with the Father and the Holy Ghost, for ever and ever. **Amen.**

(These prayers are in pre-Vatican II Benediction manuals still to be found in some sacristies.)

The Angelus

There is no doubt that a strong Marian piety has been a mark of English Catholicism in the almost two centuries since Catholic Emancipation. One widespread example is the custom of reciting the Angelus prayer – a simple reminder of the fact of the Incarnation, and the Virgin Mary's part in it, and our need for her prayers – in the morning, at midday and in the evening, these times being marked by bells. This custom is still found in some Catholic parishes, particularly cathedral parishes. The letter of Archbishop Arundel quoted above also contained a decree mandating that the Angelus should be said not just in the evening, as had been the most usual practice hitherto, but also in the morning. We do not, of course, need bells rung before we can stop what we are doing at midday to say the Angelus; but they are helpful as a reminder, and also a simple but powerful public witness to the faith.

The Hail Mary in the Bidding Prayers

Another prime instance of popular Marian devotion in England is the practice of concluding the Bidding Prayers at Mass with the Hail Mary. When, in the 1960s, questions were asked whether this was liturgically correct, Cardinal Heenan appealed to Pope Paul VI, who granted his permission for the simple inclusion of the Hail Mary in recognition of the Marian devotion of the people of England, summed up in the title the Dowry of Mary. In 1966 at their October meeting the bishops made the inclusion of the Hail Mary in the Bidding Prayers obligatory.[14]

The tradition of the Dowry recounts a story and practice of prayer and devotion that is rooted in our Catholic faith and the history of the English people, and of those who have over the centuries made their home in England.

The Message of Walsingham: The Yes of Richeldis

If we are to deepen the foundations of the Dowry tradition, it will be as a result of "contemplating the great mystery of the Incarnation" and in particular, through the story of the Annunciation. The message of Our Lady at Walsingham to Richeldis was to "share my joy at the Annunciation". This was taken to heart by the people of England. In 1893 Pope Leo XIII said these prophetic words that *When England*

---

[14] The decree states "The Hail Mary and the pause for silent prayer are to remain obligatory within the Bidding Prayers." It has never been revoked.

returns to Walsingham, Our Lady will return to England
suggesting that Walsingham is intimately associated with
the spiritual health of England. In 1983, when celebrating
Mass in Wembley Stadium, St John Paul II reflected that

> In England, "the Dowry of Mary", the faithful, for
> centuries, have made pilgrimage to her shrine at
> Walsingham. Today Walsingham comes to Wembley,
> and the statue of Our Lady of Walsingham, present
> here, lifts our minds to meditate on our Mother. She
> obeyed the will of God fearlessly and gave birth
> to the Son of God by the power of the Holy Spirit.
> Faithful at the foot of the Cross, she then waited in
> prayer for the Holy Spirit to descend on the infant
> Church. It is Mary who will teach us how to be silent,
> how to listen for the voice of God in the midst of a
> busy and noisy world. It is Mary who will help us to
> find time for prayer. Through the Rosary, that great
> Gospel prayer, she will help us to know Christ. We
> need to live as she did, in the presence of God, raising
> our minds and hearts to him in our daily activities
> and worries.

The events of Walsingham arose out of the devotion of
the Lady Richeldis, a widow who had a great desire to
honour the Mother of God. Walsingham is certainly not
the oldest Marian shrine in England, but it is the place
where Our Lady made herself known "in Spirit" and asked

for the replica of the Holy House to be built so that *all could share in the joy of my Annunciation*. The fruits of this manifestation of the Spirit brought joy, comfort and hope to all who came and continue to come on pilgrimage.

Our Lady asked Richeldis to build a replica of the Holy House in Nazareth that would be a permanent reminder of the Annunciation. Walsingham would become known as "England's Nazareth".

> It shall be a perpetual memorial to the great joy of the Annunciation, ground and origin of all my joys and the root of humanity's gracious Redemption. This came about through Gabriel's message that I would be a Mother through my humility and conceive God's Son in virginity. (Pynson Ballad[15])

Mary's request to Richeldis became her message to us, "share my joy" that her Son has become our Saviour. Richeldis's faith, and her yes to Our Lady's request, has given us in Walsingham a sacred place, a "perpetual memorial" where we are reminded to treasure all these things and ponder them in our hearts.

The Holy House in Walsingham was erected as a replica of Mary's House in Nazareth, the House of the Annunciation, where she lived with her parents Joachim and Anna. This led to England becoming known as the

---

[15] A fifteenth century versified account of the shrine's foundation. It was first published by Richard Pynson, hence its usual name.

"Holy Land, Our Lady's Dowry", and Walsingham being called the "New Nazareth":

> O England, you have every reason to be glad that you are compared to the promised land of Sion. This glorious Lady's grace and favour attest that you can be called everywhere the holy land, Our Lady's Dowry, a name given to you from of old.

> This title is due to the fact that here is built the house of new Nazareth in honour of our heavenly Queen and her glorious salutation. As Gabriel hailed her with an Ave in old Nazareth, so here that is daily remembered with joy.
>
> (Pynson Ballad)

2. Share My Joy

Some examples of Marian devotion from English Catholic history

Although many of the outward signs of Catholic life were destroyed at the Reformation, the writings and prayers of our great saints and scholars over the centuries still survive and are eloquent testimony to the depth of the devotion to the Mother of God in England.

The role and importance of joy as a pervasive attitude in English devotion to Mary is rooted in Our Lady's invitation to Richeldis to "share my joy" at the Annunciation. Here are a few examples.

St Bede the Venerable (7th Century)

St Bede, born around 672, was a Benedictine monk of Monkwearmouth Abbey in Jarrow. He was a theologian, biblical commentator, and historian. Bede is best known for his *Ecclesiastical History of the English People*, a source vital to the history of the conversion to Christianity of the Anglo-Saxons. He is the first, and so far the only, English Doctor of the Church.

My soul proclaims the greatness of the Lord, and my spirit rejoices in God my saviour. With these words Mary first acknowledges the special gifts she has been given. Then she recalls God's universal favours, bestowed unceasingly on the human race. When a man devotes all his thoughts to the praise and service of the Lord, he proclaims God's greatness. His observance of God's commands, moreover, shows that he has God's power and greatness always at heart.

His spirit rejoices in God his saviour and delights in the mere recollection of his creator who gives him hope for eternal salvation. These words are often for all God's creations, but especially for the Mother of God. She alone was chosen, and she burned with spiritual love for the son she so joyously conceived. Above all other saints, she alone could truly rejoice in Jesus, her saviour, for she knew that he who was the source of eternal salvation would be born in time in her body, in one person both her own son and her Lord.

For the Almighty has done great things for me, and holy is his name. Mary attributes nothing to her own merits. She refers all her greatness to the gift of the one whose essence is power and whose nature is greatness, for he fills with greatness and strength the small and the weak who believe in him.

She did well to add: and holy is his name, to warn those who heard, and indeed all who would receive his words, that they must believe and call upon his name. For they too could share in everlasting holiness and true salvation according to the words of the prophet: and it will come to pass, that everyone who calls on the name of the Lord will be saved. This is the name she spoke of earlier: and my spirit rejoices in God my saviour.

Therefore, it is an excellent and fruitful custom of holy Church that we should sing Mary's hymn at the time of evening prayer. By meditating upon the incarnation, our devotion is kindled, and by remembering the example of God's Mother, we are encouraged to lead a life of virtue. Such virtues are best achieved in the evening. We are weary after the day's work and worn out by our distractions. The time for rest is near, and our minds are ready for contemplation.

St Anselm of Canterbury (12th Century)

St Anselm (1033-1109), Italian by birth, was Archbishop of Canterbury from 1093 until his death. He was a key figure in the development of the doctrine of the Immaculate Conception, providing Blessed John Duns Scotus[16] (1265/6-1308) with several conceptual clarifications and insights essential for his explanation and defence of Mary's Immaculate Conception.

> The universe rejoices with new and indefinable loveliness. Not only does it feel the unseen presence of God himself, its Creator, it sees him openly, working and making it holy. These great blessings spring from the blessed fruit of Mary's womb.

> Through the fulness of the grace that was given you, dead things rejoice in their freedom, and those in heaven are glad to be made new. Through the Son who was the glorious fruit of your virgin womb, just souls who died before his life-giving death rejoice as they are freed from captivity, and the angels are glad at the restoration of their shattered domain.

> Lady, full and overflowing with grace, all creation receives new life from your abundance. Virgin, blessed above all creatures, through your blessing all creation is blessed, not only creation from its Creator, but the Creator himself has been blessed by creation.

---

[16] Scotus was Scottish, but taught at Oxford for some years.

To Mary God gave his only-begotten Son, whom he loved as himself. Through Mary God made himself a Son, not different but the same, by nature Son of God and Son of Mary. The whole universe was created by God, and God was born of Mary. God created all things, and Mary gave birth to God. The God who made all things gave himself form through Mary, and thus he made his own creation. He who could create all things from nothing would not remake his ruined creation without Mary.

God, then, is the Father of the created world and Mary the mother of the re-created world. God is the Father by whom all things were given life, and Mary the mother through whom all things were given new life. For God begot the Son, through whom all things were made, and Mary gave birth to him as the Saviour of the world. Without God's Son, nothing could exist; without Mary's Son, nothing could be redeemed.

Truly the Lord is with you, to whom the Lord granted that all nature should owe as much to you as to himself.

St Aelred of Rievaulx (12th Century)

St Aelred was an English abbot who lived during the twelfth century. He was the steward of King David of Scotland before joining a Cistercian monastery. He is famous for writing many spiritual treatises, especially *The Mirror of Charity* and *On Spiritual Friendship*. In a sermon delivered on the feast of the Nativity of the Blessed Virgin Mary, St Aelred says that everyone in the Church should honour Mary as their Mother.

> We owe her honour, for she is the mother of our Lord. He who fails to honour the mother clearly dishonours the son. Also, Scripture says: Honour your father and your mother.
>
> What then, my brothers, shall we say? Is she not our mother?
>
> Yes, my brothers, she is indeed our mother, for through her we have been born, not for the world, but for God.
>
> Once we lay in death, as you know and believe, in sin, in darkness, in misery. In death, because we had lost the Lord; in sin, because of our corruption; in darkness, for we were without the light of wisdom, and thus had perished utterly.
>
> But then we were born, far better than through Eve, through Mary the blessed, because Christ was

born of her. We have recovered new life in place of sin, immortality instead of mortality, light in place of darkness.

She is our mother – the mother of our life, the mother of our incarnation, the mother of our light... She then, as mother of Christ, is the mother of our wisdom and justice, of our holiness and redemption. She is more our mother than the mother of our flesh. Our birth from her is better, for from her is born our holiness, our wisdom, our justice, our sanctification, our redemption. (*St Aelred*, Sermo 20, in *nativitate beatae Mariae*)

Meditations on the Joys of the Blessed and Glorious Virgin Mary (13th Century)

Stephen of Sawley was a Cistercian monk of Fountains Abbey in Yorkshire. His treatise on Our Lady's Joys has a formal likeness to the Rosary; it is divided into fifteen joys, most of which are also mysteries of the Rosary, and it prescribes the repetition of the Ave Maria. Stephen's meditations echo the Rosary at a deeper level, as catechetical tools that use affective prayer to promote orthodox doctrine on the Incarnation and Mary's place in the economy of salvation. Stephen's treatise is an important antecedent to the Rosary and brings weight to the argument that English Cistercian monasticism was part of the confluence of traditions from which the Rosary emerged.

Meditation: the Annunciation

The third Joy is the Annunciation, when Gabriel "formulated the sweet salutation in which the whole world rejoices for all times to come." Here we are to "imagine the wonder, the love and joy experienced by the Blessed Virgin when the angel appeared and spoke to her, and she heard the details of the coming salvation." She alone was worthy to receive the joyful news of salvation transmitted to her from heaven by an angel.

Stephen asks her to teach us to offer to her daily "the gentle angelic salutation, this first pledge of our salvation, with a heart full of love and lips that are clean," and to grant that it may be "a comfort in all our tribulations, and a remedy in all our temptations, to her honour and glory."

Geoffrey Chaucer (14th Century)

This is part of a poem by Geoffrey Chaucer, dedicated to Our Lady, a beloved and central figure in the hearts and minds of the men and women of medieval England. It is a translation of a French original, made, tradition says, at the request of Blanche, Duchess of Lancaster, the wife of John of Gaunt.

As a non-judgemental figure of graciousness and kindness, Our Lady served as an ever-available mediator and model for believers who sought to reconcile guilt and hope. This poem is an example of the rich tradition of Marian devotion.

Almighty and all merciful queen, whom the entire world runs to for comfort and the release from sin, sorrow and pain, O glorious virgin, flower of flowers, bastion of strength and beauty, to you I flee in confusion and error. Please help and relieve me, O gentle and mighty one, and have mercy on my exhaustion and uncertainty, for my cruel adversary has overcome me.

Bounty has so firmly planted his home inside your heart that I know you won't refuse anyone who asks for your assistance with sincerity, and that you will help me, for your heart is always so generous that you are overflowing with goodwill. You are a haven of peace and refuge, of quiet and of rest. See how seven criminals pursue me! Help, shining lady, before my ship founders!

Comfort is there none in any but you, dear lady. For lo! my sin and my confusion – which it would be impolite to bring into your sight – have caused desperate charges to be brought against me, the truth of which might well justify the view that I deserve

to be damned, were it not for your mercy, O blissful
Queen of Heaven.

Sir Gawain and the Green Knight (14th Century)

The poem *Sir Gawain and the Green Knight* tells a story
from Arthurian legend. A knight takes up a challenge on
behalf of the king; the following describes where he found
his courage.

First, he has found faultless in his five senses,
and then failed never the knight in his five fingers,
and all his trust in the field was in the five wounds
that Christ caught on the cross, as the creed tells.
And wheresoever this man in mêlée was stood,
his first thought was that, over all other things,
all his strength in fight he found in the five joys
the holy Heaven's Queen had of her child;
for this cause the knight fittingly had
on the inner half of his shield her image painted,
that when he beheld her his boldness never failed.

(Stanza 28)

The Twenty-Five Joys of Our Lady (15th Century)

The Twenty-five Joys of Our Lady is an unpublished fifteenth century Middle English prose devotion preserved in the Bodleian Library in Oxford. It is presented as a vernacular Marian Rosary, the first such to be identified in the period. It illustrates the presence and practice of the Rosary itself in late-medieval England. The limited surviving evidence for the use of the Rosary in England includes woodcuts printed by Caxton and allusions in other (Latin) devotional texts.

Marie Moder, Wel Thee Be (16th Century)

This is a poem known in some fifty manuscripts, and dating originally from the fourteenth century. This is its third stanza (of twelve). The variant of the poem we give here was recorded by Richard Hill around 1504 in his commonplace book in Balliol College, Oxford.

> Mary, for your five joys,
> Help me to live a clean life;
> For the tears you shed under the cross,
> Send me grace to live life well.

St John Henry Newman (19th Century)

John Henry Newman, in 1852, gave a famous sermon called "The Second Spring". In it, he said

Something remains to be undergone, to complete the necessary sacrifice... for this poor nation's sake! But still could we be surprised, if the winter even now should not yet be quite over? Have we any right to take it strange, if, in this English land, the spring-time of the Church should turn out to be an English spring, an uncertain, anxious time of hope and fear, of joy and suffering – of bright promise and budding hopes, yet withal, of keen blasts, and cold showers, and sudden storms?

One thing alone I know – that according to our need, so will be our strength!

It is the time for your Visitation. Arise, O Mary, and go forward in your strength into that north country, which once was your own, and take possession of a land which knows you not. Arise, Mother of God, and with your thrilling voice, speak to those who labour with child, and are in pain, till the babe of grace leaps among them!

Shine on us, dear Lady, with your bright face, like the sun in his strength, O Morning Star, O herald of peace. From your sweet eyes, from your pure smile, from your majestic brow, let ten thousand influences rain down, not to confound or overwhelm, but to persuade, to win over your enemies. O Mary, my hope, O Mother undefiled, fulfil the promise of this Spring.

3. The Rededication of England as Mary's Dowry 2020

My Personal Yes

Stand at the crossroads and look, seek for the ancient paths: which was the good way? Take it and you will find rest for yourselves.

Jeremiah 6:16

The loneliness of our modern world is not eased by a superficial happiness. Hope arises from a deep well within us that is known as Joy.

And it is this joy that Our Lady offers us at Walsingham when she invites us to "share her joy." Mary was the first disciple, guiding and inspiring the Church since the beginning. She was the one who accompanied her Son from the moment of his conception at the Annunciation, standing at the foot of the cross, and present at the birth of the Church at Pentecost. This was the cause of Mary's joy, that she witnessed the events of her son and Saviour's life.

We seek after momentary happiness, but we have forgotten the meaning of joy. Joy is a consequence of knowing that we are unique because we are loved, and this love begins with God. *You called, shouted, broke through my deafness, you flared, blazed, banished my blindness; you lavished your fragrance, I gasped; and now I long for you, I tasted you and now I hunger and thirst, you touched me and I burn for your peace.* St Augustine reminds us, *you have made us for yourself O Lord, and our hearts are restless until they rest in you.*

Joy is to happiness, what the deep sea is to a puddle. Happiness, like puddles, dries up quickly. Happiness is often temporary and mostly dependent on our choices, feelings and events. Joy is like the deep sea, ever present. It comes as a consequence of accepting a gift given, and this gift never dries up. It is a form of companionship, an inner strength, that gives comfort; it is a presence, that is gentle; and as I journey through life it is the reassurance I am never alone, I rejoice, for I have accepted and taken to heart that which will never leave me.

With joy in our lives, like Mary we shall hear the words of Gabriel, *Do not be afraid Mary, for nothing is impossible for God.* Surely these are the most joyful words ever spoken, and when we take them to heart, and say our yes, we shall find the peace and happiness we so desire because we will have the joy of God in our hearts and we shall build a family and country that truly knows the meaning of peace: for it has joy in its heart.

The dedication of England as Mary's Dowry is a simple commitment to follow in her Son's footsteps, by saying Yes to him. As our forefathers and mothers did in the past, we seek her guidance and protection today. The Angelus Promise is based on the story of the Annunciation, and expresses our desire to renew our faith, so that we may serve our families, and our communities and our country, having taken to heart the words of Our Lady at Cana, *Do whatever he tells you.* (*Jn* 2:5)

The collect said at Mass on the feast of Our Lady of Walsingham lays out for us the path to follow that we may say our Yes.

Lord God, in the mystery of the Incarnation, Mary conceived your Son in her heart before she conceived him in her womb. As we, your pilgrim people, rejoice in her patronage, grant that we also may welcome him into our hearts, and so, like her, be made a holy house fit for his eternal dwelling. We ask this through Our Lord Jesus Christ, your Son, who lives and reigns with you in the unity of the Holy Spirit, one God for ever and ever. Amen.

Open your heart that you may bring him to life for others, and with Mary's prayers and protection continue to welcome him into your life, building a "holy house fit for his dwelling".

Mary, Star of the New Evangelisation

Mary, Virgin and Mother, you who, moved by the Holy Spirit, welcomed the word of life in the depths of your humble faith: as you gave yourself completely to the Eternal One, help us to say our own "yes" to the urgent call, as pressing as ever, to proclaim the good news of Jesus.

Filled with Christ's presence, you brought joy to John the Baptist, making him exult in the womb of his mother. Brimming over with joy, you sang of the great things done by God.

Standing at the foot of the cross with unyielding faith, you received the joyful comfort of the resurrection, and joined the disciples in awaiting the Spirit so that the evangelising Church might be born. (Pope Francis)

Mary *conceived him in her heart before she conceived him in her womb*. Following the example of Mary, let us take the Lord into our hearts, that we may bring him into our family, our community, our Church and our country. This dedication is a New Consecration for a New Evangelisation.

We are invited to recite the Rosary each day, "contemplating the face of Christ, seeing him – we may say – with the eyes of Mary." (St John Paul II, *Rosarium Virginis Mariae*)

St John Henry Newman reminds us that

The great power of the Rosary consists in the fact that it translates the Creed into prayer. Of course, the Creed is already in a certain sense a prayer and a great act of homage towards God, but the mysteries of the Rosary bring us to meditate again on the great truth of his life and death, and brings this truth close to our hearts. Even Christians, although they know God, usually fear rather than love him. The strength of the Rosary lies in the particular manner in which it considers these mysteries, since all our thinking about Christ is intertwined with the thought of his Mother, in the relations between Mother and Son; the Holy Family is presented to us, the home in which God lived his infinite love.

The Act of Dedication

The Act of Dedication invites you to embrace the message of Our Lady, in the Angelus, sharing her joy in the Annunciation as we follow Mary's openness to God's call, through her faith-filled "yes". Through your own faith-filled "yes", the Lord will work wonders in your life.

The Angelus Promise

V. The Angel of the Lord declared unto Mary

R. And she conceived by the Holy Spirit

As God once chose Mary to become the Mother of his Son through the message of an angel, so he chooses me this day, and invites me through the ministry of the Church or the example of another, to seek and do his will at this moment in my life.

Hail Mary full of grace…

V. Behold the handmaid of the Lord

R. Be it be done unto me according to thy Word

Mary's response to her invitation, "let it be done to me according to your Word", opened her heart to God's grace and all things became possible. Let my "yes" today take away fear, as I embrace God's will, and like Mary "ponder these things in my heart".

Hail Mary full of grace…

V. And the Word became flesh (bow or genuflect)

R. And dwelt among us

At a moment in history, Mary's faith-filled "yes" conceived him first in her heart, which then led to the birth of our Saviour. Through accepting him in my heart, enable me to recognise my role in bringing Christ to my sisters and brothers today.

Hail Mary full of grace…

V. Pray for us most holy Mother of God

R. That we may be made worthy of the promises of Christ

Let us pray:

O Holy Mother of God, pray for us, and assist us as we dedicate ourselves this day. Your yes at the Annunciation brought our Saviour Jesus into the world, and you invite us to contemplate the great mystery of the Incarnation, sharing your joy in announcing that "the Word was made flesh and lived among us." May our yes, this day, open our hearts to serve our sisters and brothers in this your Dowry, that they too may share our joy in the Good News that God walks among us. We make this prayer through Christ our Lord. Amen.

Act of Entrustment of England to Our Lady

Based on: a prayer of Erasmus (1532), Dedication of England to the Mother of God (1893), Prayer for England, Cardinal Griffin's Act of Consecration (1948), Act of Consecration by St John Paul II (1982)

Prayer O Blessed Virgin Mary, Mother of God and our most gentle Queen and Mother, look down in mercy upon England thy Dowry and upon us all who greatly hope and trust in thee.

Response We, your faithful people assembled here, offer you this country in which we live. Once it was yours, all its children were your children and you were honoured throughout England as its Protectress and its Queen. Again do we consecrate it as your Dowry, and entrust it to your maternal care.

Prayer By you it was that Jesus our Saviour and our hope was given unto the world; and he has given you to us that we might hope still more.

Response To you we entrust the Church, which invokes you as Mother. On earth you preceded her in the pilgrimage of faith. Comfort her in her difficulties and trials. Make her always the sign and instrument of intimate union with God and of the unity of the whole human race. To you, Mother of the human family, and of the nations, we confidently entrust the whole of humanity with its hopes and fears. Let it not lack the light of true wisdom. Guide it to seek freedom and justice for all. Direct its steps in the ways of peace. Enable all to meet Christ, the Way, the Truth and the Life.

Prayer Plead for us your children, whom you did receive and accept at the foot of the cross, O sorrowful Mother.

Response Pray, O Holy Mother of God, for the conversion of heart of the people of England, restoration of the sick, consolation for the troubled, repentance of sinners, peace to the departed. Queen of Peace, pray for us and give to the world the peace for which all peoples are longing, peace in the truth, justice and charity of Christ. Give peace to the nations and to the souls of all, that in peace, the Kingdom of God may prevail.

Prayer Intercede for our separated brethren, that with us in the one true fold they may be united to the supreme Shepherd, the Vicar of your Son.

Response May your prayers bring back this country to the fulness of its ancient faith. May your intercession lead us to a closer union with your divine Son. We offer you all the people of this land, especially those who know you so little or not at all. May all in our country know Christ, the light of the world and its only Saviour.

Prayer Pray for us all, dear Mother, that by faith fruitful in good works we may all deserve to see and praise God, together with you, in our heavenly home.

Response May we who follow your Son, be fruitful in the good work of building a culture of life in our world, where all human life is treasured and the gift of God's creation is respected and cared for, so that all may share the fruits of God's generous love.

V. Pray for us most holy Mother of God

R. That we may be made worthy of the promises of Christ.

Let us pray:

O Blessed Virgin Mary, Mother of God, and our most gentle Queen and Mother, look down in mercy upon England, thy Dowry, and upon us all who greatly hope and trust in thee. By thee it was that Jesus, our Saviour and our hope, was given unto the world; and he has given thee to us that we might hope still more. Plead for us thy children, whom thou didst receive and accept at the foot of the cross, O sorrowful Mother, intercede for our separated brethren, that with us in the one true fold they may be united to the Chief Shepherd, the Vicar of thy Son. Pray for us all, dear Mother, that by faith, fruitful in good works, we may all deserve to see and praise God, together with thee in our heavenly home. Amen.

The Bishop of East Anglia grants a Plenary Indulgence
to all who make the Angelus Promise on the
29th March 2020 under the usual conditions.

When we engage in good works like prayer, penance, acts
of charity, or going on pilgrimage, the Church grants a
special grace called a Plenary Indulgence. Pope Francis
explains a Plenary Indulgence thus:

> When we go to confession God forgives our
> sins, which he truly blots out; and yet sin leaves a
> negative effect on the way we think and act. But the
> mercy of God is stronger even than this. It becomes
> indulgence on the part of the Father who, through
> the Bride of Christ, his Church, reaches the pardoned
> sinner and frees him from every residue left by the
> consequences of sin, enabling him to act with charity,
> to grow in love, rather than to fall back into sin.

Plenary means that fully all the after-effects of sin that
remain within us are lifted, so we may grow through our
good acts of prayer, penance and love of others. Indulgence
means that it is a pure gift of God, given to us through the
ministry of the Church in response to our good deeds.